A Man's Life

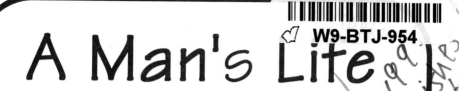

James Martin

Four Seasons Press

Classic Books for a Lifetime

Columbus · Washington DC

490347

© Copyright 1994 James Martin. All rights reserved.

Written permission must be obtained from the publisher to use or reproduce any part of this book, except for critical articles or reviews. FOUR SEASONS PRESS, PO Box 340438, Columbus, C 43234.

Library of Congress-Cataloging-in-Publication Data

Martin, James, 1945-
    A man's life / James Martin. -- 1st ed.
       p.   cm.
    ISBN 0-9642188-9-5 (pbk.) : $5.95
    1. Conduct of life. I. Title.
    BJ1581.2.M384 1994
    248--dc20   94-27683
                                 CIP

Printed in the United States of America
10 9 8 7 6 5 4 3 2 1

A Man's Life

When I began this project almost four years ago, I wanted to examine the classic and practical themes that penetrate most of our emotional and intellectual lives everyday -- and unite these philosophical quests by recognizing their existence and the influence they exerted.

The result is *nearly 140* vintage and earthly soul-searching inquiries which hold a presence in *all lives* -- such as our *adversary, death, eternity, fragility, friends, learning, love, marriage, divorce, passion, sanity, sexuality,* and... *inspiring teaching,* to name just a few.

Simple, everyday concepts we puzzle over and struggle with for a lifetime -- finally to declare -- the ultimate meanings are the ones *we* have the courage to assign them.

James Martin

Jimmy,

Do not make haste
past any one Thought,

Until you 've considered
what it has wrought.

Your

ADVENTURE

is where you see iT
and The price you pay
To geT There.

The loss of an

AdVerSarY

will be greater
than that
of a friend.

We delight

In Giving

aDvice

It relieves the burden of

accepting it Ourselves.

of **Affirmations**

There are two:

Laughter...

& Tears.

On **B**eing **A**live...

We spend our days
prepared *to be*;

Yet... in how many
of them are *we* ?

On

Appreciation

Those who have nothing,
appreciate nothing.

Argument...

or *Silence*?

Do not be afraid

of the *debate*...

Only the Hush.

**is emotion...not truth;
It is what thunders

in *your* soul.**

The Attributes:

33 from the parent comes;
33 we own ourselves.
33 never will we know.

But in the 1%,
Forever will the madness show.

Do not put your faith in

Authority;

Bullies -- all.

Blaming Parents

Let us not
fault our *Creators*
for **O**urselves.

Bluffing

Each of us can play in a game
with a hand for

deception.

Body & Spirit:

One will CRUMBLE;

yet ...One will Survive.

On Being Born

All in all,

We did not ask

to be here.

The

Bureaucrat & his **Bureaucracy**

**If a man aspires little
over a lifetime,
surely this is the place
to be little in.**

as Chemicals

If we are but the
charge between the cells,

What will we have gained
but... what can we lose?

Our Children Growing

**We hear them say
good-*b*ye in a different
way each *day*.**

Christmas

Came and went...
Staying only

with the Child.

the Compliment.....

**Do not expect praise
for doing the *unexpected or unusual*.**

Cooking up
...Companions

It may be **W**iser

to invent some friends
than to *tolerate* others.

about

Compromising:

We live day-to-day;

but-*W*oe is me...
We exit alone.

Courage

**A man of resolution
is not afraid in light--
or Shadow.**

On Curiosity

Let your claim on this Globe

be as grand as the

Universe encircling it.

The great adventure *is* obscurity;
Hence, not a moment to lose!

Should you

defend a Moron:

Please don't use your *real* name.

on _Depression_

How odd to
feel such melancholy without reason;

How lame to _f_eel at all.

DEZPERATION
& Extinction

**A hopeless heart
has good reason to
fear drowning.**

the *divinities*

When we attribute life to the gods,
What in hell do we owe
the heavens?

D-i-v-o-r-c-e

that certain recognition
by each party

of the *Other's*

imperfections.

real**D**rama

Spews theater

from the first day..

To the final *hour.*

Dreams & Aspirations...

"Ahh..." to discover
the will and the way
to fuel our vision!

On Dying

**We do not depart unaccompanied
when we are loved.**

Education

What can be taught
without the experience of
knowing it exists?

Effort

Where we begin doesn't matter much;
Where we attempt to go does.

When**E**ntering:

A **GRAND** entrance
does not always guarantee
the grand treatment.

Entertainment

By the way,
Haven't you found
a fun spot
by now?

theEntrepreneuR

One who *o*wns
his own business

is **K**ing of **p**urgatory.

O_{ur} *Errors*

are personal matters--

Not moral issues.

Eternity

I am never more amazed
than to equate our lives

With the infinity before birth —

and the one after our leaving.

human **EVOLUTION**

FOUR billion years
of evolution...and it's still just

You and me.

Existence

& Longevity

The stars and we live out our lives
in due course, or else suddenly explode...

...leaving *Stardust* particles
to form *a*new.

Expectations

Count on nothing **each Day,**

exclusive of <u>**Your**</u> **own offering.**

our *Universal*

Experience...

**Is it not possible to live
in a corner...**

yet dwell in the CENTER of the Universe?

Animals near

EXTINCTION

Are

Our 10 **largest** creatures--
all hunted by **man.**

FAIRYTALES

We believe in children's stories
when the old men
write them.

Farewell,

I will offer my goodbyes
to them *all* -- but
lo n **g** before *my* departure.

my Father's Advice

In our final conversation:

*"**D**o what makes you happy*
that which gives you joy."

Faults

I am more familiar
with *your many*
than **my few**!

Good Feelings

Hold **O**n to **m**arvels and **W**onders;

Do not let any go.. **U**ntil the last flash.

THE **F**INITE **V**S

THE **I**NFINITE

We live in a world
of limited mentalities, forever
clogging endless possibilities.

the *f*ollowers...

Bring on your henchmen,
and your hangers-on;

mental masturbators... everyone.

royal *Food*

The inmate's **B**READ and **W**ATER

Is more fit
than most have imagined.

ishFOOlness

If not for the ABSURD
We say and do,

Humanity and I
would be a bore...and

Just perhaps, you too.

Forgiveness

When you finally pardon those
you can, you have earned
the right to forget them.

Fragility:

Not one of us is less delicate
than the other; we simply shatter
in different places.

a FRIEND

The *enemy* can't betray us;
Such is the province
of the familiar.

the *Coming Generation:*

By each and every act we let--
True through time:
the *next* shall get.

A **God**

for the moment,
is the **O**ne
who saves a stranger.

Happiness

OBSERVED

A life of relative happiness
is enough.

In search of a Hero

Will you find one better--
than in your own home?

Take the *High Road*

Even *A*lone,
it's more appealing

than the low road...
available to us all.

Hunter *and.......... the* Hunted

Brave *man*: afraid of
no squirrel, rabbit or
deer unarmed.

under the

*I*NFLUENCE*S*...

Some of our lives
live on very well

without us.

Inner Workings:

We learn more about ourselves
when we have no crowd
to *cheer* us on.

Insanity

Creeps *silently*

in...then out of our lives
each day -- Thank god.

Insecurity

The unsure path
is the sure path.

Insight

I have discovered more intuitiveness

into the nature of things

in the **g**round below --

than the earth above.

Being

Interconnected

We <u>may</u> be related,

but hardly Interchangeable.

Once Intimates

**When my companions
took their leave,**

**I did not attempt
to replace them.**

The Journey......

Where all we go

We come again....

Knowing the Other:

**After all these years,
I can tell you:**

No **one sees anyone.**

Laughter

fails none of us.

from the Learning tree

We are what we have **p**icked--
And what we have *dropped*.

Our
Life Lived

The experience we create
Is **the book we write.**

Listening...

Have we
not been taught

how?

*L*ove &

*D*edication

**To be devoted
to the *interests* of a person
Is to share love.**

Maintenance

We are no more
than our daily effort.

MAMMALS

Remember, the giant Whale

**and the tiny Shrew
are not *unlike* the other.**

Marriage

Is fueled
by hope and lust;

Who would believe
the two could rust?

No

Measurement

Can define

the value of a
Man, Woman, or Child.

Are *echoes,*

calling forth a past

We need never deny.

THE MISER

Is known for what he does
not give, more than
for what he hoards.

Mom and *Dad*

I would like to know
My Mother's heart
My Father's marrow.

In the Moment

We spend our Days *moving*
from the *past* to the Future

... *but* Who are we
In the twinkling of an eye?

Money & _its_ Value

May be measured
by how much is used,

When we are making _none_.

Beware of the **Monsters** who

guard the gates to the gold;
They will kill you
slowly, and in degrees.

Morality

A virtuous crutch
cannot support
its flock for long.

MOTION
& T I M E

Neither time
***nor* mankind**
move *noticeably*.

when doing it

My Way

Few, if any, do
what *I think* is right.

Nature

is neither

a prostitute nor a Courtesan;
and has no need for
public attention or private debate.

pondering Obscurity

*N*o one realizes

he has left
the auditorium.

There is n0 kinder gift

than an **Old Friend**

to ring you up with an

offering of his time.

Hopefully,

our lives are worth
more
than their

Origins.

Parasites

*F*eed off our vision
and resources,
until they are swatted away...
or squashed.

Parenting

*T*he able from both sides
must eventually
be let go.

We may have many

Passions

but... **O**nly *one* 1Over.

The Past

Turn away where pain
and irritation reign,

But *embrace the* insight.

A
petty Life
is its own reward.

The Philosopher

Contemplates

The meaning of the *universe*...
and the meaning of a *flower*.

Prejudice

will always hide from
its own failures.

Prodigy

vs the Venturer

Is the man of genius greater than the man constructing *layers* of achievement and triumph at his *own risk*, *one* block at a time?

(Think again.)

RacingWith Ourselves

We do not win
when we run alone;

We do not lose either.

on Recognition..

To be obscure
Is to be secure.

THE REFERENCE

When we are who we say we are...

We do not require proof.

Reflection &

Memory...

Layered in moments, then years;

**Brought forth in dreams
and quiet places.**

mere Religions

**The idea of Obscurity
is simply *too* much for most
to endure *too* long.**

Being

Remembered

We are never quite recalled...

Or ever quite forgotten.

Respect

To be *well thought of*
may at times may be better
than being desired.

*your***B***rain at* **Rest**

W hen in doubt:

N_{ap}.

A *Retrospective*

**Live *your* life that
you will look back on it**

And s m i l e!

At the **REunion**

**We come together
to unite our *former* self
with the *one* in the present...**

When you seek

Rules:

to accompany the journey,

your destination

has thus been chosen.

personal Salvation

the ha**r**dest person
to save *i*s
You.

The Two Seasons

Winter

holds us hostage;

Spring,

allows us to breathe.

Self-learning

What we discover

ON OUR OWN

**endures beyond
what we are taught
by most others.**

Separation of

Children

We need not miss them when they are content.

onServing

A man whose duty is to *himself* and *family*, advances Mankind.

male SeXuality

**Has not *yet* equaled
that of the *F*rog.**

Simple Vs Complex-Minded

**No one is as constipated
as he may appear.**

Or,

**as exaggerated as he would
make you believe.**

Solitude

Thriving alone,
We have found Seclusion;

Pain from aloneness, and
We have discovered
our *isolation*.

Solution
vs Problem

The solution should
never be *more* difficult
than the problem.

Song of Life

When you
find your song,
will you
keep singing?

Stranger and the Mate

**It is not *uncommon*
for the *outsider* to be treated
more kindly than the spouse.**

*S*uccess

**Can be measured
by what we can offer ourselves —**

and a *few* others.

an Inspiring

TeaCHeR

Is worth Three
mediocre parenTs.

Shed a new ***T****ear...*

each day,

for all who have come --

then passed away.

Time & Value:

Above all else,

Treasure the moment,
and those you spend it with.

On *T*IPPING

**No gratuity is too large
or too small..**

Until you ask for change.

TRANSITIONS:

to **O**ld

We are *there* when there is

Nowhere else to be.

The Ultimate

Understanding:

You, I *comprehend*

It's *me* I'm *not* sure of.

A Union of Equals:

Grants not Victories...

Yields no Victors.

M*aterial* V*alue*

**The weight of
all we own is light;**

**It can be signed away
by** *Signature.*

WAITING

The line drew 'round the world

Knowing *not* for what...
sighing breathlessly:

"I'm next!"

Wealth

**You do not seek fortune;
You do not let it escape.**

The source of *Well being...*Seldom comes from another; Found, it dwells inside.

Wisdom

Does not follow;
it only leads.

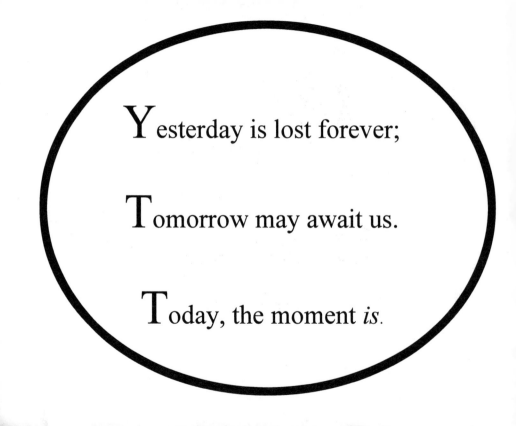

Yesterday is lost forever;

Tomorrow may await us.

Today, the moment *is*.